CRANES

Dan Osier

PowerKiDS
press™

New York

For Tristan Yip

Published in 2014 by The Rosen Publishing Group, Inc.
29 East 21st Street, New York, NY 10010

First Edition

Editor: Amelie von Zumbusch
Book Design: Andrew Povolny
Photo Research: Katie Stryker

Photo Credits: Cover, pp. 11, 17, 19 iStockphoto/Thinkstock; pp. 5, 9 AlexKZ/Shutterstock.com; p. 7 LittleStocker/Shutterstock.com; p. 13 Apostrophe Productions/Workbook Stock/Getty Images; p. 15 Artit Thongchuea/Shutterstock.com; pp. 21, 23 Dmitry Kalinovsky/Shutterstock.com.

Library of Congress Cataloging-in-Publication Data

Osier, Dan.
  Cranes / by Dan Osier. — First edition.
    pages cm — (Construction site)
  Includes index.
  ISBN 978-1-4777-2863-5 (library) — ISBN 978-1-4777-2957-1 (pbk.) —
ISBN 978-1-4777-3034-8 (6-pack)
  1. Cranes, derricks, etc.—Juvenile literature. I. Title.
  TJ1363.O85 2014
  621.8′73—dc23
                              2013023113

Manufactured in the United States of America

CPSIA Compliance Information: Batch #W14PK3 For Further Information contact Rosen Publishing, New York, New York at 1-800-237-9932

Contents

Cranes 4

Working with Cranes 12

Kinds of Cranes 18

Words to Know 24

Websites 24

Index 24

Cranes are tall! They lift loads up high.

You often see them on job sites.

The long part of a crane is the boom.

Some cranes have **outriggers**. These help them not tip over.

The **operator** sits in the cab.

The rotex gear is under the cab.
It lets the cab spin around.

The **signalman** tells the operator where to go.

Crawler cranes have tracks instead of wheels.

19

Tower cranes are very tall. They are set in concrete.

21

Do you like cranes?

23

WORDS TO KNOW

operator   outrigger   signalman

WEBSITES

Due to the changing nature of
Internet links, PowerKids Press has
developed an online list of websites
related to the subject of this book. This
site is updated regularly. Please use
this link to access the list:
www.powerkidslinks.com/cs/cranes/

INDEX

C
cab, 12, 14

O
operator, 12, 16

T
tracks, 18

W
wheels, 18

24